SAGiTTARiUS

SAGiTTARiUS

23 November–22 December

PATTY GREENALL & CAT jAVOR

MQP

Published by MQ Publications Limited
12 The Ivories
6–8 Northampton Street
London N1 2HY
Tel: 020 7359 2244
Fax: 020 7359 1616
Email: mail@mqpublications.com
www.mqpublications.com

Copyright © MQ Publications Limited 2004
Text copyright © Patty Greenall & Cat Javor 2004

Illustrations: Gerry Baptist

ISBN: 1-84072-763-2

1 3 5 7 9 0 8 6 4 2

Printed in Italy

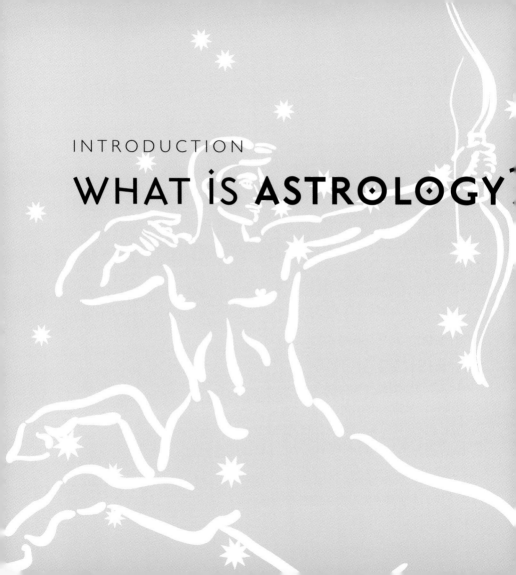

INTRODUCTION

WHAT IS ASTROLOGY?

Astrology is the practice of interpreting the positions and movements of celestial bodies with regard to what they can tell us about life on Earth. In particular it is the study of the cycles of the Sun, Moon, and the planets of our solar system, and their journeys through the twelve signs of the zodiac— Aries, Taurus, Gemini, Cancer, Leo, Virgo, Libra, Scorpio, Sagittarius, Capricorn, Aquarius, and Pisces — all of which provide astrologers with a rich diversity of symbolic information and meaning.

Astrology has been labeled a science, an occult magical practice, a religion, and an art, yet it cannot be confined by any one of these descriptions. Perhaps the best way to describe it is as an evolving tradition.

Throughout the world, for as far back as history can inform us, people have been looking up at the skies and attaching stories and meanings to what they see there. Neolithic peoples in Europe built huge stone structures such as Stonehenge in southern England in order to plot the cycles of the Sun and Moon, cycles that were so important to a fledgling agricultural society. There are star-lore traditions in the ancient cultures of India, China, South America, and Africa, and among the indigenous people of Australia. The ancient Egyptians plotted the rising of the star Sirius, which marked the annual flooding of the Nile, and in ancient Babylon, astronomer-priests would perform astral divination in the service of their king and country.

Since its early beginnings, astrology has grown, changed, and diversified into a huge body of knowledge that has been added to by many learned men and women throughout history. It has continued to evolve and become richer and more informative, despite periods when it went out of favor because of religious, scientific, and political beliefs.

Offering us a deeper knowledge of ourselves, a profound insight into what motivates, inspires, and, in some cases, hinders, our ability to be truly our authentic selves, astrology equips us better to make the choices and decisions that confront us daily. It is a wonderful tool, which can be applied to daily life and our understanding of the world around us.

The horoscope—or birth chart—is the primary tool of the astrologer and the position of the Sun, Moon, Mercury, Venus, Mars, Jupiter, Saturn,

Uranus, Neptune, and Pluto at the moment a person was born are all considered when one is drawn up. Each planet has its own domain, affinities, and energetic signature, and the aspects or relationships they form to each other when plotted on the horoscope reveal a fascinating array of information. The birth, or Sun, sign is the sign of the zodiac that the Sun was passing through at the time of birth. The energetic signature of the Sun is concerned with a person's sense of uniqueness and self-esteem. To be a vital and creative individual is a fundamental need, and a person's Sun sign represents how that need most happily manifests in that person. This is one of the most important factors taken into account by astrologers. Each of the twelve Sun signs has a myriad of ways in which it can express its core meaning. The more a person learns about their individual Sun sign, the more they can express their own unique identity.

ZODIAC WHEEL

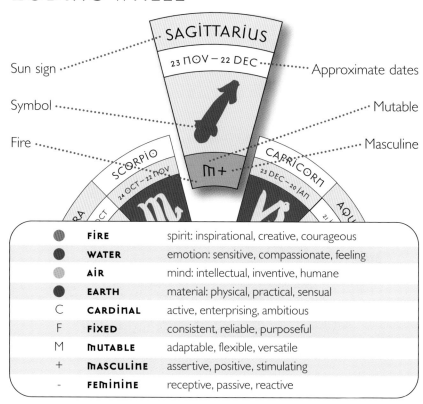

Sun sign ········· SAGITTARIUS

Approximate dates ········· 23 NOV – 22 DEC

Symbol ·········

Mutable ·········

Fire ·········

Masculine ·········

SCORPIO · 24 OCT – 22 NOV

CAPRICORN · 23 DEC – 20 JAN

M +

●	**FIRE**	spirit: inspirational, creative, courageous
●	**WATER**	emotion: sensitive, compassionate, feeling
●	**AIR**	mind: intellectual, inventive, humane
●	**EARTH**	material: physical, practical, sensual
C	**CARDINAL**	active, enterprising, ambitious
F	**FIXED**	consistent, reliable, purposeful
M	**MUTABLE**	adaptable, flexible, versatile
+	**MASCULINE**	assertive, positive, stimulating
-	**FEMININE**	receptive, passive, reactive

ARIES
21 MAR – 20 APR

TAURUS
21 APR – 21 MAY

GEMINI
22 MAY – 21 JUN

CANCER
22 JUN – 22 JUL

LEO
23 JUL – 22 AUG

VIRGO
23 AUG – 22 SEP

LIBRA
23 SEP – 23 OCT

SCORPIO
24 OCT – 22 NOV

SAGITTARIUS
23 NOV – 22 DEC

CAPRICORN
23 DEC – 20 JAN

AQUARIUS
21 JAN – 19 FEB

PISCES
20 FEB – 20 MAR

C+   F-   m+   C-   F+   m-   C+   F-   m+   C-   F+   m-

PART ONE

THE ESSENTIAL
SAGITTARIUS

RULERSHiPS

Sagittarius is the ninth sign of the zodiac and the third Fire sign after Aries and Leo. It is ruled by the planet Jupiter and its symbol is the Centaur Archer, half-horse and half-man, in the process of taking aim with his bow and arrow. This symbol represents the sign's dual nature—baser animal instincts combined with higher human and spiritual aspirations. Sagittarius is a Mutable and Masculine sign. There are earthly correspondences of everything in life for each of the Sun signs. The part of the human body that Sagittarius represents is the thighs. Gemstones for Sagittarius are topaz, turquoise, blue zircon, and amethyst. Sagittarius signifies stables, fields, hills, and the highest points of mountains, and, in the home, the fireplace. It also signifies hunters, clergymen, broadcasters, and philosophers, as well as all things foreign, travel, dreams, visions, and wisdom. It is also associated with birch trees, olives, and lime flowers, as well as higher education and university.

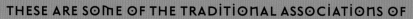

THESE ARE SOME OF THE TRADITIONAL ASSOCIATIONS OF

SAGITTARIUS

The part of the human body that Sagittarius
represents is the thighs.

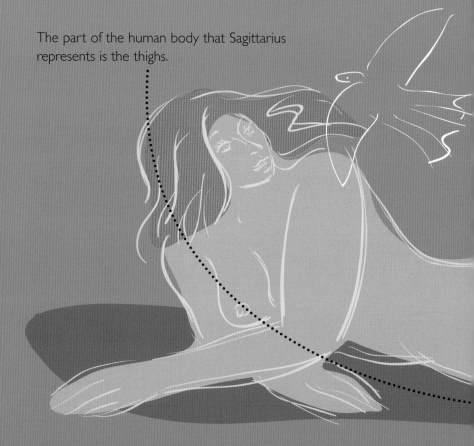

lime flowers, birch trees

the highest point
of a mountain

PERSONALITY

The boundless warmth, curiosity, and optimism of the Sagittarius individual is like a beacon of positive energy to those who get bogged down in their own personal concerns and problems. This sign is all about elevating the mind, lifting the spirit, and expanding the horizons of knowledge and experience beyond the confines of accepted normality.

There's always an element of the teacher or guru residing in the heart of even the wildest Sagittarius. Even if they don't consciously go out of their way to enlighten or inform others about the many subjects that intrigue them, Sagittarians have a natural ability to engage people's interest and inspire them to think along unfamiliar lines. The world view of a Sagittarius is very different from that of almost everyone else. They see life from a holistic perspective, with all things connected and, as a result, they reject nothing but try to find a place in the big picture for everything. They don't concern themselves with the petty details of how it all fits together, only with the imperative to leave nothing out and to include everything in their vision.

Of course, all Sagittarians have their blind spots, but these in themselves become their motivation for their never-ending voyages of discovery. They are always open to more learning, knowledge, and experience; it's as if they were trying to chase away ignorance and misunderstanding. They are philosophical enough to know that it's quite impossible, in one lifetime, to see all there is to see, know all there is to know, and experience all there is to experience, but that doesn't seem to stop them from trying. Sagittarians are intrepid travelers on land, sea, and air; they enjoy going to strange and foreign lands, where they can engage fully in new cultures. A Sagittarius passport makes very interesting reading; it's bound to be full of entry and exit stamps from many different countries.

However, it isn't only the wonderful vistas along the highways and byways of this planet that draw their attention; they find journeys of the mind equally seductive. Sagittarius thinkers will immerse themselves in the ideas and philosophies that emerge from all the information that they absorb and will explore, without prejudice, things that go beyond physical experience and into the realms of pure concept. Indeed, when they go in the search for answers to difficult questions and their thoughts are traveling along a particularly convoluted path, you need to shout loudly to get their attention for, at moments like these, they can be oblivious to the world around them.

Sagittarius is an expansive sign and its natives seek to increase their experience, knowledge, and anything else that they can lay their hands or hearts on. Because of their far-reaching enthusiasm and their need to stretch way beyond normal human expectations, they often appear larger than life and over the top—which is how they end up getting to the top or, at least, to the edge. These are people who dare to push back boundaries, and in doing so, reap the rewards. They can also be idealistic, but somehow they usually manage to keep their thoughts and impulses within the bounds of reality. However, this isn't always so, for where there's a will, there's a way.

Almost everything Sagittarians do, they do in a big way. Even when they lose their tempers, they do it so that they almost explode; unfortunately for those around them, that fiery temper has a way of unleashing a volley of well-aimed verbal arrows. The aftershocks reverberate for a long time after they've forgotten all about whatever it was that got them angry in the first place. But Sagittarians hold no grudges, do not brood, and do not harbor bad feelings; they are quick to forgive and will move swiftly on to the next thing that catches their attention. Nor are they petty or small-minded; it's the big picture that interests them. Their temperament may occasionally be volatile but they have a very buoyant nature and will bounce back from any setbacks and glide over the minor annoyances of life with ease.

Sagittarians have restless minds, bodies, and souls; they're never content to stay home for there's such a lot of world to explore and so much future to embrace. Feelings of being caged in or trapped by responsibility, whether toward a lover, family, friends, or property, are unbearable to the free-spirited Centaur. It's not that they refuse to do their bit; they don't mind joining in and getting their hands dirty, but when their bit becomes a monotonous routine that keeps them tied or tethered to one spot, then a very grumpy and unhappy Sagittarius is the result.

Freedom of movement and thought are the ultimate pleasures of all those born under this sign. They love to go off and take part in sporting activities in the great outdoors, with the wind blowing through their hair and oxygen pumping through their lungs. If they keep on moving, then they can continually find new positions from which to view the world and this will protect them from predictability and stultifying boredom.

Sagittarians are famed for being optimists, although some would argue that their optimism has a touch of the unreal about it. However, it is well known that optimism attracts good luck; negative attitudes may protect people from disappointment but a positive outlook opens the doors to the greatest opportunities. If you dare to believe, your dreams can come true and that's just one of the many reasons why Sagittarians succeed at the most extraordinary feats. Abundant Jupiter, a most wonderful protector and provider, is Sagittarius's planetary ruler, so it's in their nature to expect the best and to allow the worst to roll off their shoulders. Sagittarians are fortunate, jovial individuals; they are truly inspired and are quick to inspire others.

CAREER & MONEY

Just because Sagittarians appear to take things lightly, it doesn't mean that they don't know how to handle a serious deal when they have one. Although they sometimes seem happy-go-lucky, make no mistake, they're certainly nobody's fool. Their double-bodied zodiacal sign—half-human and half-beast—means that they represent the perfect blend of wild and cultured. When it comes to their career, it's true that they'll take risks, but those risks are carefully calculated ones.

Sagittarians are masters of making something of nothing in many different spheres, but in relation to business and careers, this is a very valuable gift. They have a boundless capacity to grow, create, and thrive, and they know how far to go, when to strike, and when to hold back. They also have a good sense of what is and isn't possible. They'll take longer leaps than most other people would dream of taking, but then most people don't even attempt to reach their full potential in the way that Sagittarius does. There's the possibility that Sagittarians may suffer burnout, since they're always burning both ends of the candle, but they find that the only way to make sure that all corners have been covered is by throwing light into them.

When they need time out, they'll take plenty of it and they'll dig in deep to recharge their batteries, but when they're back, it's with such vigor and passion that they're bigger and better than before. Ever expansive and always on the move, Sagittarius is the ultimate upwardly mobile person. And when it comes to checking out the byways that they find unexpectedly on the bends in the road, they are meticulous; no stone will be left unturned.

Their aimless, sometimes reckless image is only a cover; it's there to highlight their untamed side. But they're ace Archers, always keeping their eye on the target and rarely making the mistake of seeking glory from their shots at success. For Sagittarians the journey counts just as much as reaching the destination.

When it comes to money, Archers are very relaxed; being ruled by Jupiter gives them a lucky streak so they often have an easy-come, easy-go attitude to material possessions. If they have money in their pocket, then they'll spend it, and quickly, but if there isn't any, then they don't worry. They're pretty sure that one day soon, one of the many ventures they're involved in will bear fruit and will help them to pay off all of those boring bills. They have a talent for allowing the practical, mundane things in life to slide, and why not? There's a world out there waiting to be discovered and it might yield all kinds of treasure.

With their love of freedom, it's no surprise that Sagittarians can often be found in professions that give them plenty of it; these include working as pilots, racing-car drivers, writers, researchers, or in careers in the travel industry or in higher education. Above all else, Sagittarians need to do their own thing—and they do it so well!

THE SAGITTARIUS **CHILD**

Almost from birth, little Sagittarians have an exuberance about them. They kick their little legs and thrash their arms about so that it's almost impossible to keep them tucked up snugly and securely in their blankets. They get so much exercise when they're tiny that it's no surprise that their little muscles are strong enough for them to start walking earlier than most other children. Once they can move about under their own steam, there had better be some safety gates around to stop them escaping. They're such natural explorers that, given the chance, they'll wander about the house getting into every room, closet, and drawer. And as they get bigger, the sofa is bound to get a bit of beating; they just love turning somersaults on it. They'll also know every inch of the garden and local park like the back of their hands; the Sagittarius child is constantly drawn to uncharted territory.

Their fun-loving enthusiasm means that they make popular playmates at school and they love getting involved in team sports and usually do very well in any competition. But their interests don't stop at physical activities; they enjoy poring over picture books, particularly illustrated dictionaries and encyclopedias. That's one pastime that's guaranteed to keep them sitting still for quite a while, although it won't be a quiet time for those around them because they like to talk about all the interesting things they're reading about. Everything will excite their hungry minds, from the animal kingdom, religion, and science to travels in foreign lands and space travel.

As they grow into adolescence their desire to head off and experience the big wide world firsthand may mean that they don't pay enough attention to the practicalities of schoolwork and education. It may be possible to convince them that concentrating on the subjects that inspire them at the same time as gaining a good grounding in the ones that don't, is part of their preparation for the adventures that lie ahead. All in all, their natural good humor and delightful high spirits make them very pleasant people to have around.

PERFECT **GİFTS**

Sagittarians are active in mind and body. They're also goal-orientated and they like a challenge. They enjoy sport, particularly football and archery, as well as gentler sports such as croquet and badminton. A gift consisting of a sentimental memento will do little to interest them, no matter how carefully it's been thought about. They may keep it in order not to hurt the giver's feelings but they really would prefer something with more pizzazz.

It's not easy to offer Sagittarians something to wear; firstly because, since Sagittarius rules the thighs, they're into skirts and trousers and it's difficult to buy those for someone else and, secondly, because they can be particular about their clothes. However, you can't go far wrong with a gift that has a foreign twist. They'll always appreciate an Indian shawl, an Oriental bag or belt, or a piece of jewelry from the Middle East.

If you're in search of something less personal, a reference or travel book will intrigue them for hours and, if you can afford it, they'd definitely make the most of a short break abroad or a night in an exotic hotel.

FAVORITE **FOODS**

Sagittarians enjoy jovial conviviality. They love to visit restaurants that specialize in foreign cuisine with a bunch of their friends, and they'll usually choose pretty adventurous dishes from the menu. Their choice will often be spontaneous, depending on what they fancy at that particular moment, but the method of preparation and the herbs and spices used must be authentic. Sagittarians have a sweet tooth, but exotic herbs and spices also tickle their taste buds so they like the flavors of cinnamon and nutmeg added to their sugar. They have no particular preference as to which region of the world provides their favorite fare; each has its specialties, and Sagittarius will be very well-versed in all of them.

When they're cooking for themselves, Sagittarians are imaginative and far from predictable. They often produce meals that can only be described as fusion food—bold, unusual combinations of flavors from different regions of the world. Often in a rush, Sagittarians love to start the day with a potent shot of caffeine, usually made from a special blend of their own invention or from handpicked coffee beans from some secluded plantation in Brazil. They often eat on the run, so you'll frequently find sandwich wrappers or takeout containers stuffed in their briefcase, lying around the floor by their desk, or stashed in the side pockets of their car door. But they'll consume at least one meal in the day, however simple, with relish, though with which particular relish—tomato, onion, or mango—is anyone's guess.

FASHION & STYLE

Take even the most classic, designer-dressed Sagittarius and you'll find a little hint of the exotic about them, some radical twist or splash of color that shouts, "I'm no uptight square!" It may be the beaded Native American belt or the Indian silk scarf that gives the game away and lets everyone know that this person is either well-traveled or is into "global chic." The most important thing for every Sagittarius clotheshorse is that they have freedom of movement; they hate feeling restricted in any way by too-tight trousers or a too-small jacket and they like to feel that what they're wearing is appropriate to what they're doing.

You'll always find a good selection of casual clothes in their closet, and often they'll be clothes of the athletic or sporting variety—track pants, sweatshirts, and trainers, for example. Sagittarians don't wear them solely for trips to the gym; they find them useful for pottering around the house and garden, walking the dog, or for trips to the market. Ask any Sagittarius and they'll also tell you that there's nothing better for comfort on a long-haul flight.

They enjoy dressing up as well, and usually do so with exceptional style because they have a knack for knowing what suits them. Blues and purples usually look best on them, but so do the sandy tones of far-off deserts and beaches or the khaki of the modern warrior. They can wear bold, colorful patterns but these are best kept to a minimum or reserved for accessories.

İDEAL **HOMES**

Enchanting and full of intrigue, the Sagittarius home has style and panache, the kind that draws people in and gets them looking around as though they were casing the place. Their homes have so much to look at, but they're far from cluttered. The objects that the Archers choose to put on display all reflect their personal philosophy, their passion for exploration, and for seeking out new experiences. This is a message that beguiles everyone, whatever their age, filling their guests with the same kind of wanderlust that exists in the heart of every Sagittarius.

Designing a home comes very naturally to Sagittarians. They don't really go out of their way to make it into a picture of perfection, but they have a knack for throwing things together so that somehow they end up working well. And they know how to complete the look, often by adding something with a foreign motif. All in all, they appreciate other cultures and could easily adapt to the lifestyle of somewhere quite unlike that of the place where they were raised.

PART TWO

RISING SIGNS

WHAT IS A RISING SIGN?

Your rising sign is the zodiacal sign that could be seen rising on the eastern horizon at the time and place of your birth. Each sign takes about two and a half hours to rise — approximately one degree every four minutes. Because it is so fast moving, the rising sign represents a very personal part of the horoscope, so even if two people were born on the same day and year as one another, their different rising signs will make them very different people.

It is easier to understand the rising sign when the entire birth chart is seen as a circular map of the heavens. Imagine the rising sign — or ascendant — at the eastern point of the circle. Opposite is where the Sun sets — the descendant. The top of the chart is the part of the sky that is above, where the Sun reaches at midday, and the bottom of the chart is below, where the Sun would be at midnight. These four points divide the circle, or birth chart, into four. Those quadrants are then each divided into three, making a total of twelve, known as houses, each of which represents a certain aspect of life. Your rising sign corresponds to the first house and establishes which sign of the zodiac occupied each of the other eleven houses when you were born.

All of which makes people astrologically different from one another; not all Sagittarians are alike! The rising sign generally indicates what a person looks like. For instance, people with Leo, the sign of kings, rising, probably walk with a noble air and find that people often treat them like royalty. Those that have Pisces rising frequently have soft and sensitive looks and they might find that people are forever pouring their hearts out to them.

The rising sign is a very important part of the entire birth chart and should be considered in combination with the Sun sign and all the other planets!

THE RiSiNG SiGNS FOR SAGiTTARiUS

To work out your rising sign, you need to know your exact time of birth—if hospital records aren't available, try asking your family and friends. Now turn to the charts on pages 38–43. There are three charts, covering New York, Sydney, and London, all set to Greenwich Mean Time. Choose the correct chart for your place of birth and, if necessary, add or subtract the number of hours difference from GMT (for example, Sydney is approximately ten hours ahead, so you need to subtract ten hours from your time of birth). Then use a ruler to carefully find the point where your GMT time of birth meets your date of birth—this point indicates your rising sign.

SAGiTTARiUS WiTH **ARiES** RiSiNG

When Aries is the rising sign, the fiery, energetic qualities of the Sagittarius personality are even more evident. These people live life in the fast lane and often appear as if they're on a mission to see more, do more, and experience more than anyone else. They're so enthusiastic and they don't let any opportunity pass them by. They tackle everything head-on regardless of whether they have what it takes to pull it off. Mostly they're successful but sometimes they fall flat on their faces in the attempt. That doesn't worry these Sagittarians in the slightest; they simply pick themselves up, dust themselves off, and start all over again—while keeping an eye open for the next opportunity. And if that just happens to be halfway across the world, well, never mind! As ever, they'll be chasing their dreams and grasping them with both hands. Friends and family won't even try to keep up with a Sagittarius with Aries rising as they seem to change course so often, so it's probably best to wait and let them come back in their own good time.

SAGITTARIUS WITH **TAURUS** RISING

With Taurus rising Sagittarius is very calm and steady. These people appear totally laid back and relaxed; nothing seems to faze them. The only thing that's quick about them is their open, generous laughter. However, it would be wrong to assume that they're in any way slow or easy to take advantage of; they see everything and miss nothing, and often surprise others with their insightful comments. There's much more to these individuals than meets the eye. They may look subtle on the outside but that conceals a massive inner reserve of strength and passion. Great lovers of luxury, these travelers probably have antique Louis Vuitton luggage that they picked up years ago in a thrift store for a song. They are the "bons vivants" of the Sagittarius clan and could happily while away many hours in pleasant surroundings in the company of good friends, drinking wine and telling stories. They're also beguilingly sensual people whose most intimate relationships are intensely physical. There's a mystique about them that draws people in, but at the same time, they enjoy helping others delve into the heart of their own affairs. The Sagittarius with Taurus rising would benefit enormously from the help of other people in terms of cash or connections.

SAGITTARIUS WITH GEMINI RISING

With Gemini as its rising sign, this Sagittarius is even more of a "people person." These Sagittarians are usually found rushing from one meeting or get-together to the next. "Places to go and people to see" is something you'll often hear them saying. They find it almost impossible to stay still or be on their own for very long; loneliness is to be avoided at all costs, yet they're not exactly frightened of being alone. Their quest is to find out who they really are by measuring themselves against others. They don't do it for competitive reasons; they just need to gauge themselves and define who they are. They are quick to form close relationships because they need that type of symbiosis in order to develop, as well as to help others. But they could never be called "dependent;" they don't depend on others any more than others depend on them. One reason that they flit about so much is that they value their freedom and independence so highly that they never stay in one place long enough to get tied down. Terribly chatty and very clever, they're popular people and are loved for their ability to lift everyone's spirits and make witty jokes.

SAGITTARIUS WITH **CANCER** RISING

These are most lovable Sagittarians because, with Cancer rising, they have the sensitivity and empathy that makes others feel comfortable and secure in their company. They are enthusiastic, but they also have the ability to tune into other people's needs and are genuinely caring when someone requires their assistance. They won't go around looking for people in distress but when they hear a cry, they won't hesitate to find out what they can do to help. Cancer rising gives these individuals a quieter, more reserved appearance than other Sagittarians, and they also tend not to give much away about themselves. Although they can be boisterous and high-spirited, they often prefer to sit back and observe other people, using their intuition in their quest for greater understanding of the human condition. At work, they're ambitious and conscientious and have a wonderful ability to order information from many disparate sources into a personal world view that will assist them in whichever career path they choose. They're often drawn to working in healthcare where they can use their talents for making a difference to other people's lives on a directly personal level.

SAGITTARIUS WITH **LEO** RISING

This is one flashy, exciting individual! The Sagittarius with Leo rising will stand out head and shoulders above a crowd. These people have a lust for life that is open and freely expressed, added to which they have a touch of class and a sense of the dramatic. They're warm, generous, and fun-loving and are often the life and soul of a party, always making sure that everyone is in high spirits and feels welcome and involved. They're also glamorous, sexy people-magnets who, by the sheer force of their confidence and charisma, naturally gather others to any cause or project that they're involved in. They speak loudly and clearly, and are given to making large gestures and sweeping movements. Some quieter people will steer away from them because such a big, all-encompassing presence can be a little daunting. Sagittarians with Leo rising are generous, magnanimous souls, but they also seek reassurance and the acceptance of others. It might look as if they're sometimes full of themselves, but the fact is that they can be as uncertain as anyone, especially when they're criticized. But they do love life and people, and people usually love them in return.

SAGiTTARiUS WiTH **ViRGO** RiSiNG

It may take Sagittarians with Virgo rising a while to feel confident enough about themselves as individuals to come out and show who they really are, but once they do, it's clear that they're fun-loving and have a lively, comic sense of humor. At first, in the company of people who aren't their nearest and dearest, they appear reserved and serious, but once they become part of a crowd, they express themselves warmly and usually with a great deal of accurate intuition, which others find very inspiring. They're strongly influenced by their family, who offer the protective shield that keeps them coming back home, but as they grow, they seek to form their own base from which to operate. They have an excellent understanding of the workings of the world, both from a global and a personal perspective, and they usually keep on top of mundane matters such as paying bills and household repairs. They like to organize their lives so that they run as smoothly as possible and so that they have the time and space they need for mental rumination and for the travels into their consciousness that feed their hungry souls.

SAGITTARIUS WITH **LIBRA** RISING

This is the international businessperson *par excellence*! With Libra rising, Sagittarius gets the refined, genial manners that are so important when dealing with people from other cultures, plus a keen eye that spots quality and a good deal. They could do well out of the import and export of desirable luxury goods, but even if they themselves have no interest in buying and selling, they have a natural ability to attract other people to it. Others are always interested in what Sagittarians with Libra rising have to say and the lively, enthusiastic way in which they say it. They could also make great travel writers and inspiring teachers. In fact, these clever, witty, and charming individuals are so talented and quick to learn, that they might try their hand at almost anything, provided that there was no danger of it becoming tedious. They are excellent communicators, quickly comprehending a given situation and accurately conveying information about it to others in a most pleasing, sometimes musical way. In fact, they enjoy and are good at being the mediator, bringing people together through their ability to balance both sides. Usually, the Sagittarius with Libra rising is beautiful to look at and a delight to listen to and manages to combine a wry sense of humor with an optimistic outlook on life.

SAGITTARIUS WITH **SCORPIO** RISING

♏ The highly perceptive Sagittarians with Scorpio rising often have an intense look in their eyes, as though they are studying every nuance and subtlety in the people or subjects that they feel warrant their scrutiny. These Sagittarians have a penetrating mind that enables them to get to the bottom of an issue, a motivation, or perplexing problem with laser-like accuracy. Indeed, they can become so focused on something that they automatically block out every distraction. Very self-controlled and willful, they always have a purpose in mind and will steadily apply their quiet effort to it, finding creative ways around any problem or obstacle. They enjoy the company of others but aren't usually the life and soul of the party. These Sagittarians prefer deep, meaningful intercourse along philosophical lines, and usually with just one other person. They're excellent at handling money and they know it, but they run the risk of identifying themselves too closely with material possessions. They need to learn that valuing themselves for their innate talents is what will lead to a more fulfilling and successful life; they can then, very easily, turn those talents into great financial rewards if they wish.

SAGITTARIUS WITH **SAGITTARIUS** RISING

Rambunctious and ready for anything, double Sagittarians are very inspiring people indeed, even when they don't mean to be. They light up a room simply by walking into it and they spread their warmth and goodwill to whomever happens to be there. They always seem to have a smile on their faces, even when the chips are down, for they know that they'll always end up on top or, at worst, alright. With their positive outlook on life, they willingly take up challenges and seize opportunities as though they were no big deal. They often find themselves with so much on their plate that they have no choice but to throw themselves at it with gusto. There's also always something new turning up in their lives; they're so open to what the world has to offer in terms of experience and adventure that they never have time to worry about being cautious or looking before they leap. Despite this, they seem to attract good fortune with ease; they have well-tuned instincts as well as an uncannily lucky touch that is bestowed on them by Jupiter, their planetary ruler. It will always help to see them through any hiccups.

SAGITTARIUS WITH **CAPRICORN** RISING

Sagittarians with Capricorn rising can be strange, complicated individuals. On the one hand, they seem to move freely through life, happily and patiently taking things as they come; yet on the other, they appear to apply their efforts to things in a rather conservative manner, achieving great success from every goal they strive for. They seem, as if by magic, to attract the things in life that they need. These people aren't easy to read, for when they're in one of their many playful moods, you can never be quite certain that their raucous laughter is aimed at the same thing as everyone else's. They certainly arouse people's interest and curiosity but they can be impossible to figure out. They have a philosophical approach to life that is, in fact, very practical because it helps them to know instinctively which endeavors are worth their continued effort and attention and which aren't. If some project doesn't have a chance of reaching its potential, then they'll move on to the next one. Highly imaginative, they have the ability and energy to make their dreams come true, but their aspirations lie beyond any of the material status symbols that they invariably collect on their way.

SAGITTARIUS WITH **AQUARIUS** RISING

With the sign of Aquarius rising, the Sagittarius individual has an idealistic, revolutionary, and rebellious streak. These Sagittarians are the radical, anarchist, freedom-loving champions of the people. There'll be a touch of the merry bohemian about them, for they enjoy the company of unusual, even eccentric, people from all walks of life. In fact, their life is like an adventure that leads them on a quest to save the world, or at least a small part of it, for they will attempt to make their own particular microcosm a better place, with the people in it getting along as equals and feeling mutually fulfilled. These individuals have a powerful need to belong to a truly global society, and would love to see all national boundaries torn down so that everyone in the world could wander freely and without prejudice. That's their philosophy, at least. On an everyday level they come across as friendly, excitable, and likable, with clever, inventive minds and a need to be valued members of a group of like-minded people. Generally, they are very broad-minded and accepting, and they need others to feel the same about them.

SAGITTARIUS WITH **PISCES** RISING

Warm, gentle, kindhearted Sagittarians with Pisces rising may appear to float about aimlessly but somehow they always seem to rise to the top. They possess a type of effortless ambition—or at least that's the way that it seems to other, less lucky, people. But these Sagittarians have a method to their madness; although they don't appear to be ambitious, they need to secure their place in the world and be respected for what they do as much as for who they are. They have an incredible ability for sensing when the right opportunity comes along, and they waste no time in getting on board. They are extremely intuitive, passionate, and caring toward those they love. They are usually gentle, but can be boisterous and they know how to have a good time when they're out on the town. They are philosophical and understanding, mysterious and complex; it's often very difficult to know what they're thinking and, in most cases, any guess would be wrong, for their minds and spirits travel through realms that have never been traveled through before. Their slightly exotic looks mean that people often mistake their nationality.

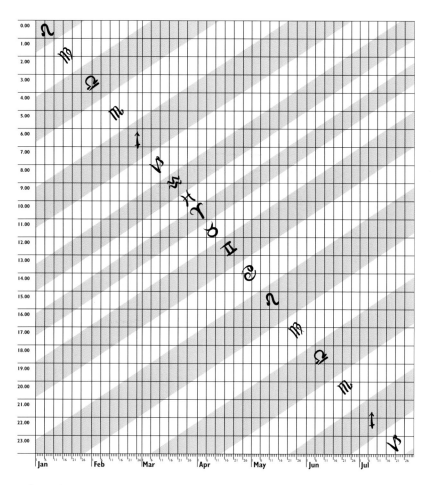

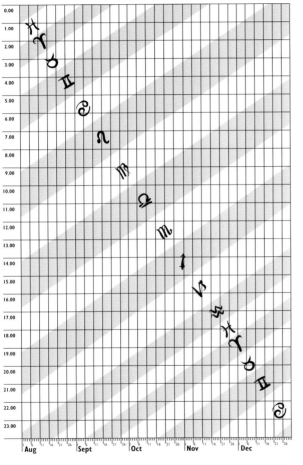

rising sign
CHART

New York
latitude 39N00
meridian 75W00

♈	aries	♎	libra
♉	taurus	♏	scorpio
♊	gemini	♐	sagittarius
♋	cancer	♑	capricorn
♌	leo	♒	aquarius
♍	virgo	♓	pisces

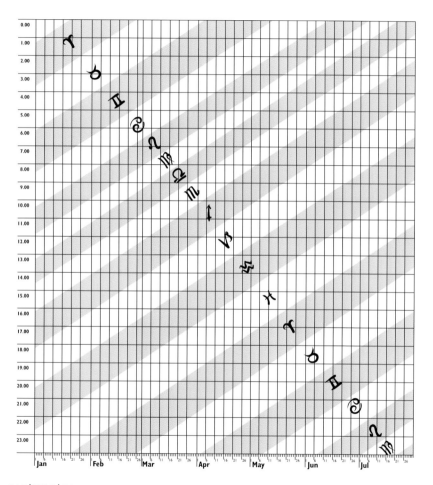

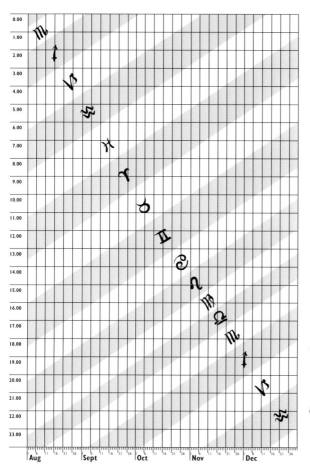

RISING SIGN
CHART

Sydney

latitude 34S00
meridian 150E00

♈ aries	♎ libra
♉ taurus	♏ scorpio
♊ gemini	♐ sagittarius
♋ cancer	♑ capricorn
♌ leo	♒ aquarius
♍ virgo	♓ pisces

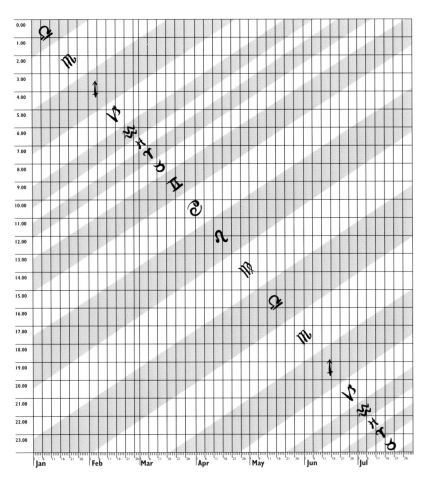

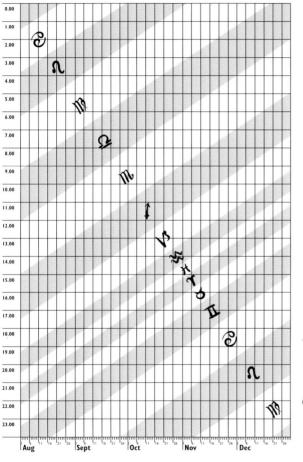

RISING SIGN
CHART

London
latitude 51N30
meridian 0W00

♈ aries	♎ libra
♉ taurus	♏ scorpio
♊ gemini	♐ sagittarius
♋ cancer	♑ capricorn
♌ leo	♒ aquarius
♍ virgo	♓ pisces

PART THREE
RELATIONSHIPS

THE SAGITTARIUS **FRIEND**

It's hard for anyone to resist exuberant, optimistic, fun-loving Sagittarians, particularly when they are in full swing and up for a few laughs. Their natural warmth and inclusive nature simply gather people up to join in the jovial adventure, even if that means nothing more than sitting and having a chat. They make wonderful raconteurs with their tall stories and funny anecdotes, and enjoy being the life and soul of the party. However, they don't hog the limelight; they encourage others to open up and express themselves freely.

Because they usually lead busy lives, dashing about here and there, they might not always be available for regular social get-togethers, so any club where they're counted on once a week won't suit them. Sometimes months, or even years, can go by with no word from them. People who want to stay in touch had best leave a trail that Sagittarius can follow in order to reestablish contact. But they never forget a good time or a friendly face and will appreciate a call or an unexpected visit when they're back home, fresh from their voyages of discovery. Then they'll be happy to pick up where they left off and will regale any listener with wonderful stories of their travels.

Disagreements don't faze them; in fact, ten minutes later, they probably won't remember having had one at all! Nor do they bear a grudge; life's too short and there's so much fun stuff to do, so why waste time on that?

SAGITTARIUS WITH **ARIES**

These two Fire signs get on like a house on fire but their raucous slapstick behavior could wear down the tolerance of friends and family alike so they'll need to tone things down if they want to keep their other friends. Aries and Sagittarius are like-minded yet Sagittarius can enhance the spiritual awareness of Aries, and Aries never fails to stimulate the inquiring Sagittarius mind. It's all action, energy, and enterprise when these two are together. Like children, they can play for hours on end and get up to all sorts of mischief. If tempers flare, sparks and flames will fly, but they're both quick to forgive.

SAGITTARIUS WITH **TAURUS**

Sagittarius is never short of bright ideas. This intrigues Taurus to begin with, but when Taurus really wishes to follow up one of the ideas, Sagittarius is unlikely to treat it seriously and this will annoy Taurus, who doesn't take too well to flippancy. These two signs could both respond to a new plan with equal amounts of passion, but then they'll proceed in different ways. They might end up having a very productive relationship and working in tandem, but generally speaking, there's little common ground between them. Sagittarius is a wide-ranging traveler, while Taurus is most comfortable at home or kicking back and relaxing. However, in small doses, this friendship could work well.

SAGITTARIUS WITH GEMINI

The Twins and the Archer are opposite one another in the zodiac and the result could be one of two things—love or hate. Sagittarius takes the long view while Gemini sees the immediate surroundings. Together they could conquer the world or they could end up walking different paths entirely. Both have a slapstick sense of humor and really know how to have fun. Other people will have to beware as pranks and practical jokes will abound when these two are together. But when they get serious, Sagittarius will probably ignore the lightheartedness of Gemini, which is what makes Gemini tick, and Gemini will dismiss the philosophy according to Sagittarius.

SAGITTARIUS WITH CANCER

Cancer loves to hear stories of faraway places and far-fetched possibilities and could listen to a glittering Sagittarius tale of adventure the entire day. Quite simply, they are fascinated by the Archer's seemingly inspired life story. But the Archer won't be so impressed by Cancer, except by the fact that Cancer admires them! Sagittarius is prone to flattery but Cancer is actually genuinely interested in Sagittarius, so much so that they could almost be persuaded to leave home for a short time in an attempt to have some similar adventures. This friendship isn't about regular contact; it's more about enjoyable accidental encounters.

SAGITTARIUS WITH **LEO**

When these two first spot one another, a big smile will come to their lips; both will be thinking "Hooray! Let's go and play!" as they immediately feel a warm sense of fun. Each is good at building up the other, too, though they won't be constantly complimenting one another; somehow they naturally spur the other on to enjoy the game of life in their own special way. Theirs is the kind of friendship that says, "We're great together, so let's show the world!" They make a lifelong, happy-go-lucky pair of friends, and even if they do have the occasional argument, neither will hang onto it or even mention it again.

SAGITTARIUS WITH **VIRGO**

This is a quizzical friendship that may take a while to develop. Both will find the other interesting and pleasant enough, but they won't necessarily arrange to get together again unless they share a common hobby or interest. If they do, then repeated exposure to one another will mean that they gain a great deal from the other's special talent or particular perspective. They have much to offer one another but it will take some time for them to recognize this fact. Once they do, then they will make plans to meet up, but this will be for a dose of interesting information rather than for some company.

SAGITTARIUS WITH **LIBRA**

The wide-ranging philosophical bent of their Sagittarius friend is an exciting enigma to Librans who occasionally need lessons in detachment in order to fly free with their ideas. Librans, meanwhile, are perfect playmates and they make ideal, encouraging companions for Sagittarians, who long to relate to them on an intellectual level. Not only that, but they'll both love going out together, getting some fresh air, and being active. They'll make great friends and they'll also find that they offer the other enough of a challenge to stretch their minds.

SAGITTARIUS WITH **SCORPIO**

This is a revealing and enlightening friendship and, like a good thriller, one that's hard to put down. Conversations between Scorpio and Sagittarius go deep and have a mind-expanding effect. Both have a way of getting the other interested and intrigued. However, while exploration of ideas and experience is their baseline, both have very different ways of approaching it. Sagittarius wants to head out on the town for spontaneous fun and action, while Scorpio would prefer holing up in the corner of an interesting bar or bistro and observing the action at the same time as giving a wry running commentary on it.

SAGITTARIUS WITH **SAGITTARIUS**

When these two wisdom-seekers get together, then something truly enlightening is sure to happen. They'll never tire of listening to each other's tales of adventure and will spur each other on to such wild, exciting behavior that things could get out of hand if they weren't so wise to the ways of the world. Rip-roaring and raucous, these two great friends are able to enjoy a pure, unadulterated friendship that's open and stimulating for all concerned. It's only when they go quiet on those around them that people know that they're cooking something up—perhaps a practical joke.

SAGITTARIUS WITH **CAPRICORN**

These two could be very good friends, particularly if they have a joint project that they both want to see completed. They'll inevitably find themselves joining forces on some issue or other because they get a real charge out of the way that their conversations start with nothing more than a good idea and end with the solid foundations of an excellent plan of action. Sagittarius helps Capricorn to see the lighter side of life, while Capricorn helps Sagittarius to take things a little more seriously, but they're not friends simply in order to be on a learning curve. They actually like each other and know that they're good for each other because what one lacks the other has, and vice versa.

SAGITTARIUS WITH **AQUARIUS**

These two have the ability to excite and inspire each other's imagination and, what's more, they'll have a good giggle at whatever those imaginations manage to concoct. They share an easy camaraderie because they accept each other at face value and wouldn't presume to pass judgment on the other. Theirs is a live-and-let-live-and-then-let's-laugh-about-it approach to life. Sagittarius's wild and wonderful streak combined with Aquarius's wacky but groovy twinkle makes a convivial combination. Combine that with the unexpected new discoveries that they make every time they meet and there's enough in it to keep them friends forever.

SAGITTARIUS WITH **PISCES**

As friends, these two really click. They can share boundless fun when they're out on the town together. They have a way of daring one another to do really audacious things, and if their mothers only knew what they were up to, they'd be ordered home immediately! On the other hand, with their two heads together, they could accomplish great, courageous feats. Their conversations can be silly or serious, but what's sure is that they'll both enter into them in the right spirit. They even find their arguments enjoyable because they'll expand each other's perspective with their different takes on life. Both having a jovial and generous streak, these two are an inspiration to one another and make great pals.

THE SAGITTARIUS WOMAN iN LOVE

With her sparkling eyes and devilish grin, the playful Sagittarius woman isn't afraid to show her passionate feelings for the man she desires and/or loves. She's lively and lusty and has a healthy appetite for sensual indulgence. Although she's often considered promiscuous, it would be a mistake to believe that this woman isn't capable of devoting herself to the special man in her life. It's true that she needs her freedom, but it's also true that once she's found the man who'll bestow the gift of love and trust on her, she'll love him with all the dedication and tenderness that her big heart can offer. The love she needs is pure and simple, devoid of the jealous, suspicious, and possessive feelings that often accompany romance, but she needs to be embraced with as much love as she offers others.

It's true that she does like attention and can be a bit of a show-off, especially when she's with friends and deep in verbal banter, but who doesn't like to be noticed, especially by the opposite sex? She's attractive, fun-loving, and full of life, and only wants to express her sense of enjoyment, so if her man finds her flirting with someone else, it would be best if he celebrated her vivacity and love of life alongside her, rather than try to quash it. The Sagittarius woman has a need for adventure and her partner should be able to share in this endeavor. She's not a house mouse; in fact the phrase "domestic bliss" probably conjures up scenes of horror in her mind.

Actions speak much louder than words for her. She's open and demonstrative with her feelings and such gestures mean far more to her than empty promises. Somewhere in the heart of the Sagittarius woman lies the fear that she may never find a partner who will wholly satisfy her need for a limitless, uplifting, and always-exciting romantic relationship. But she's not a perfectionist and would welcome any man who came close to perfection in her estimation, so when Mr. Right does walk into her life, she'll know it; she's intuitive.

She can also be proud, however, so any little slight could make her back off for good. She may appear flippant and, at times, superficial, but those traits mask a generously loving soul who is just as vulnerable to pain as anyone else. She may laugh it all off in public but she's sensitive and knows that she deserves more than to be belittled; she should only be adored.

Any man who wants her must also realize that it's vitally important to keep her interest. She has a hunger for knowledge, especially for knowledge of new and intriguing aspects of her lover that she could explore. The Sagittarius lady is exciting and stimulating, and her enthusiasm and dynamism are very infectious. In return, she requires spontaneity, wit, and intelligence from her man, as well as loads of physical, sexual passion.

SAGiTTARiUS WOMAN WiTH **ARiES MAN**

In love: The Aries man will respond perfectly to the Sagittarius woman's infectious optimism. These two lovers will probably always be rushing around town, having fun here, thrills there. It would be a wonder if they ever had the time to stop and look dreamily into each other's eyes. Forget dreamy. This relationship is fiery hot and scorching with sex appeal. They have so much in common and are both so passionate about life. They want to experience everything and go everywhere, and they'll just love being able to do it all together. If they really "click," then they'll also be able to coordinate their need to be on their own sometimes so that no time is wasted when they are apart. However, life together could get so hectic that they'll both constantly brush problems under the carpet and end up tripping over the bumps! But that's hardly a reason not to be together. There is far more in common between these two than not, and any dating agency would naturally put them together because they are so similar in their aims. Their mutual, insatiable sense of adventure will never be exhausted, so long as they both shall live. Their romance may not be of the traditional kind, but there will be no less love between these two passionate Fire signs than there is between any lovestruck pair. They just have a different way of showing it, that's all. But they both know it's there, even when they're fighting—and that's not such an uncommon occurrence as they also love to make up!

In bed: This is a gluttonous combination of delights — a serious pleasure-fest involving the love-hungry Aries man and the Sagittarius woman with her huge appetite for enjoyment. Just one piece of advice: a round of lovemaking between these two could last a long time, so with all the sweating they'll be doing while exploring each other's pleasure zones, they'll need to drink plenty of water. And while they're in the kitchen getting it, they should also grab the whipped cream, some honey, a few grapes, and some oysters, and make it a real feast! Once the relationship gets started, they can cancel their gym memberships because they'll be getting the best workout possible right there in bed! The Aries man is an exciting lover, open to anything, and he won't be able to get enough of his Sagittarius temptress. There's just so much to try out, and her flair for foreign trends could see her belly dancing, acting the demure geisha, or performing the can-can, all of which will drive him mad with anticipation. She'll love his attention and he'll be totally immersed in her vision and variety. She's generous to a fault and he'll quickly learn to give as good as he gets. He has the energy and initiative to keep her quivering with excitement. They won't want to let each other go, and there's really no need. Between them there will be nothing but their big hearts.

SAGITTARIUS WOMAN WITH **TAURUS MAN**

In love: One thing to remember with this combination is that the Taurus man prefers his woman to stay by his side, and that of all the signs, Sagittarius is the one with an insatiable wanderlust. The

Taurus man will be possessive of his Sagittarius lady and will want to keep all of her adventurous energy for himself. And although she is attracted to his obvious masculinity and sensuality, she's a girl who really can't be pinned down or caged in. She will love and respect the Taurus man and is capable of being loyal. Equally, he will love and respect her, as long as she abides by his rules. It's likely that her love of wide, open spaces and uncharted territory is a little too wild for the domesticated Taurus guy, yet her optimism and cheery personality give him a charge that puts a bemused smile on his face. For all his rigid demands, this is one woman the Taurus man might make an exception for. She would love having this powerful, steady man to come home to, and to take care of all life's practicalities while she takes off on her various voyages of discovery. The problem is that he's not the type to be happy allowing her out of his sight, and eventually, that might mean that she's happier not coming home at all. These two people really like each other, but some compromise will be necessary in order to keep the relationship firing on all cylinders.

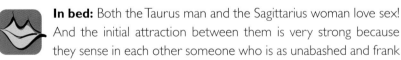 **In bed:** Both the Taurus man and the Sagittarius woman love sex! And the initial attraction between them is very strong because they sense in each other someone who is as unabashed and frank about their sexual desires as they are. When they get it together, sex could be raunchy, definitely very physical, and oddly satisfying. He will love the way she navigates herself around his body with her hungry curiosity, and she can't help but lose herself in his intense masculine strength. They will both

respond with an equal amount of ardor and fervent passion, and indeed, if they're willing to work at it, they could build up an intense little inferno in the bedroom. There could be just one problem: while the tenacious Taurus man isn't at all work-shy and is happy to persist in the pursuit of pleasure, the Lady Archer needs more immediate results. Her attention is capable of waning, while he can stay focused for long periods of time. She can be ready for it anytime, anywhere, and she enjoys the spontaneous adventure. He, however, wants it in a big, comfortable bed, at around bedtime, which means that, in the long run, sex could get a little too predictable for her taste. Compromise and negotiation are key factors in keeping this love alive. If she can have her way for half the week and he for the other half, this sexual union could provide a very colorful array of scrumptious erotic choice.

SAGITTARIUS WOMAN WITH GEMINI MAN

In love: Excitement and adventure meet and meld in the Gemini man and Sagittarius woman relationship. Nothing is ever dull when the two of them are together. They can make anything fun, even an argument! Whether they're chatting in a café, dancing till dawn, or making love on a beach, they just know that their partner is enjoying it as much as they are. They're opposites who exert a fatal attraction on each other. Here is a woman who can give the freedom-loving Gemini man a taste of his own medicine. She leads an active life and follows her own interests with a singular intent. She's warm and generous and would embrace the idea of him joining her at any time, but he shouldn't expect her to hang around and beg him to get involved. That's what he'll love about her; she takes life as it comes. More often than not he'll want to join her on her spontaneous adventures and invite her along on his, so these two will often be found trucking around together, laughter ringing out and music blaring. They can travel optimistically through life, never letting its more serious side get them down. And as they'll never get bored with each other, it's unlikely either will find a good reason to finish it. Such a great relationship is hard to find, especially for two such free spirits. Even if they do wander away from one another, it won't be too far or for too long.

In bed: The Sagittarius woman will love the way he quivers when she touches him and, knowing how quickly her passionate energy gets going, he'll become transfixed as he dances his fingers all over her bare skin. And so it goes both ways with these two. Both enjoy constant stimulation—mental, spiritual, and physical. Making love is a highly charged experience that will leave their bodies fulfilled and tingling with cosmic love. With her insatiable adventurous spirit, the Sagittarius woman will enjoy exploring Gemini man's body: he's totally responsive as she discovers previously uncharted territory. And this is one woman who isn't afraid to boldly go where no woman has gone before; she's uncannily accurate in her guesses as to what will get the Gemini man's sexual energy going. It's as though his thoughts and desires fly like arrows straight into her mind. As a Lady Archer, she knows just how to handle the arrow of lovemaking and is well practiced at hitting the bullseye. He, on the other hand, knows how to feed her fire so she can keep climbing to the peak, but he does chatter so, which can be a little distracting, so she might have to climb all night to reach the summit. But there's so much sexual energy between these two that they might as well be going at it throughout the night. It's near impossible for them to keep their hands off one another, even while asleep!

SAGITTARIUS WOMAN WITH **CANCER MAN**

 In love: These two don't really appear to have much in common so this could be regarded as a very strange coupling, but what one lacks, the other makes up for. Together, they could make something that is close to a whole—well, near enough! The good thing is that they both have such different perspectives on life that there's always a chance they could learn something valuable from each other. Although they may get on each other's nerves once in a while, they can also love each other and, to some degree, tolerate one another's foibles, and this can keep them together through thick and thin. Basically, the Cancer man's heart is where his home is; this is where he goes to get his security fix before he goes out and faces the big, wide world. By contrast, the Sagittarius lady's home is where her heart is—wherever that may be at any given time. She loves to get out in the world, seeking knowledge and vision and only coming home for a change of clothes. It could be tricky for these two to find a middle ground but if they combine hearts and homes, they could just hit it off. At worst, his moods will drag her spirit down and her tactless, offhand comments could hurt him badly. As long as he's employed outside the home rather than working from it, he won't get too clingy every time she wants to head out the door. And, if there are good planetary aspects between their personal horoscopes, there's certainly some hope.

In bed: Initially, the attraction between these two could be very strong and sexy. The Sagittarius lady will sense Mr. Cancer's brooding sexuality and she is always prepared to try anything once. He may find a few steamy nights of hot and heavy sex rather sweet, but unless she can offer him a token of her commitment, he may simply back away into his shell. She's a wild one and he'd love to be with her, but he won't be sure of himself when he's around her. He'll always wonder whether he measures up to her more adventurous style. Sure, he can try to tie her down, but she won't like it because she wants to have fun in the bedroom and any restrictions would simply put her fire out. The Cancer man is very emotional and he needs to feel secure with his partner or else he gets crabby. Will she be able to react appropriately? She's very sexually, if not emotionally, tuned-in, so at least her lusty passion will give him a modicum of contentment, but he could begin to feel like a sex-object after a while. Most men would revel in this, but if the Cancer man feels he's only appreciated for his abilities in the bedroom, he'll eventually get depressed. An agreement to have an on-off relationship would keep the heat on high with this couple, but that may be a bridge too far for the commitment-seeking Cancer man.

SAGiTTARiUS WOMAN WiTH **LEO MAN**

In love: The Leo man is magnetic and charismatic, and when he makes those grand, extravagant gestures to show her just how much he loves her, the Sagittarius woman simply melts. These two individuals are on the same energetic vibration. They really understand each other and, because that understanding runs so deep, there's great potential for true love. He's the center of attention wherever they go, and she just loves to be right alongside him since he attracts such unique and interesting people into their circle. He's proud to have such a worldly, accomplished, and fun-loving woman with him. Their spirits can really soar when they spend time together and each will inspire and encourage the other to fulfill their true potential. When they both have the same goals, the creativity that this partnership can generate is awesome; they make a wonderful team because she can spot the opportunities and he can bring the grand schemes to fruition. However, there are a few hurdles to jump first. The Leo man can be extremely demanding but she remains unfazed by it, which is probably for the best since it keeps his ego in check—and he'll recognize this fact. On the other hand, the Sagittarius woman's need for freedom and spontaneity could cause him some problems; he expects to be the center of her world at all times and his territorial nature could make her feel restricted. But, if she gives her Lion plenty of love and attention, he'll give her the universe! And that's what she really, really wants!

In bed: He's spontaneous, sexy, and very passionate—and so is she! Both the Leo man and the Sagittarius woman have very healthy sexual appetites. Indeed, they may find themselves in bed together very often—no matter what else they should be doing. She brings out the beast in him and he brings out the best in her. With her passions unleashed, the Sagittarius woman feels free to be the desirable sex goddess that she really is! And for once in his life, the Leo man doesn't feel that he has to tone down his voracious appetite. It thrills her to know that with him she can be uninhibited and adventurous, and that his passion is as hot and unrestrained as her own, and yet he can still bring out the soft and most feminine aspects of her nature. He makes her feel like a lady, no matter where they are or what the circumstances. She's a lady whose sexual motor is running on full throttle and if she really wants to make his engines roar, then she should put on her expensive underwear, add a dab of her most exquisite scent, and serve him the best champagne in the finest crystal glasses. This highly refined behavior will certainly bring out the animal in him. He'll want to devour her all night!

SAGITTARIUS WOMAN WITH VIRGO MAN

In love: This is a complicated coupling but it's not impossible. The Virgo man loves the Sagittarius lady's adventurous soul, but persuading him to go along with her would be like trying to teach him to be footloose and fancy-free—it's simply not something he does.

However much spontaneity appeals to him in theory, in practice he feels the pull to remain grounded. Trying to tame the Sagittarius woman would be like trying to domesticate a tiger; there's a wild side to her that must remain free to range wherever her soul leads. He admires her optimism, but at times he attacks it with his cynical humor. His cleverness and ability to organize all the practical issues of daily life will attract the Archer lady; that's what she needs, in fact, so he's very good for her. Her attention is so often focused on the big picture that she trips herself up on the little details that he is so skillful at tidying away. Love may grow, but she'll have to tend it well if she wants it to flower, since his nerves may not be able to take too much of her wild unpredictability. Unfortunately, there's a chance that they'll both be so caught up in doing their own thing that they'll forget to merge their interests, and once they let the relationship slide, they'll have a difficult time getting it back. On the plus side, at a mental level this is a great partnership. She's the one with the wicked sense of humor and he's the one with the dry wit. They love to laugh together and will do so often.

In bed: The Sagittarius lady will love the ardor and bliss that the Virgo man offers between the sheets. This man might be from the element of Earth but he can certainly match her fire with his physical passion. It's definitely in him to get very involved in the sexual process but if she wants to release that bubbling erotic energy that he keeps so well hidden, it will take some persistent effort. She doesn't usually see the point in being subtle when it comes to expressing her lusty desires, but if she's hunting a Virgo then the game is more one of hide-and-seek than kiss-chase. He needs to remember to focus on the whole woman, not just on the sweet bits that he finds so delectable. Time will probably show that though this relationship is good in many ways, in the end, it may lack the right kind of friction. They'll certainly be able to enjoy games in bed but it's the daytime antics that threaten to spoil the anticipation of the night's excitement. Their individual methods of seduction just don't seem to spark the ignition without a little tinkering to get their motors running. But if the Sagittarius lady likes to travel and can go the extra mile with her Virgo man, then he'll definitely take the brakes off.

SAGITTARIUS WOMAN WITH **LIBRA MAN**

In love: From the moment when they first meet, the Libra man will charm the Sagittarius lady. He'll see all that's exciting and beautiful in her, and will make it his mission to attract her attention so that he can tell her all about it. He'll wine and dine her and woo her with so much romanticism that she simply can't refuse him, and why would she? This man has everything she could ever want, and might even give her the earth if she asked for it. Even a more rough-and-ready Libra man will bring out her feminine side and make her feel like a heroine in a romantic novel. These two will enjoy being together at parties, in restaurants, walking along a moonlit beach, in the bedroom, anywhere. They have such an easygoing rapport that it seems as though there's something running through their blood that supplies them with enough action, fun, and adventure to keep their hearts burning with desire for one another. There'll be no temper tantrums or violent scenes between these two, because when they put their heads together, they can work out almost any problem. Except perhaps one: the Sagittarius woman needs the freedom to come and go as she pleases, while the Libra man needs the two of them to do everything together, so he might want to tag along even when it's not appropriate. Love and friendship come easily to these two and it can be a long-lived and ideal partnership as long as they keep the channels of communication open.

In bed: At first, the Sagittarius woman's lovemaking is free and easy, and bright and breezy, but the more she warms up, the more wild and abandoned she becomes. The Libra man is very giving and wants her to have a good a time, so he'll do all he can to fan her flame into a passionate inferno, while she could be just the *femme fatale* he needs to ignite a fire in him that he never knew he had! He more than responds to her adventurous, lusty expression of sexuality; it makes him feel as though he's riding high on love when the Lady Centaur looks at him with burning desire in her eyes. She'll carry him far beyond the edge of his expectations. He's had the fantasy, now here's the real thing! But she must behave in a ladylike fashion, which is not always easy for a woman whose unleashed passion can make her howl like the wildest of animals. And that's the only catch in this coupling; he's all man and possesses a powerful libido, but he has romantic ideas about how love should be expressed. Although he likes his

Sagittarius woman to be feral and free, he also wants her to be sweetly mysterious and feminine. That's a bit like asking a wild horse to take part in a dressage routine. If he wants to keep her, he'll need to find his inner animal to match hers.

SAGITTARIUS WOMAN WITH SCORPIO MAN

In love: When the Scorpio man focuses his laser-like intensity on the hard-to-get Sagittarius woman, he'll make her squirm in a most delicious way! She can sense danger and excitement and she's a sucker for a challenge. He, meanwhile, is fascinated by everything about the adventurous Sagittarius woman. This is a life puzzle that neither participant can wait to solve and both long to follow the titillating road of discovery that leads to each other. She is open and bold about it, while he is secretive and prone to reading too much into everything. However, they share a fascination with life and all its deeper and higher meanings, so their spiritual connection is likely to be very strong. The downside is that half the time, living with the Scorpio man will be like walking on eggshells because he's so sensitive; the spontaneous Sagittarius woman, who prefers to just get on with things, could find it all very draining. They're both on their own paths and going in different directions, so in time, their paths may no longer cross and the distance could get too great between them. The good news is that both are searching for a deeper, more thorough understanding of the world and when they compare notes, they'll find the feeling's mutual. Most encouraging of all, of course, is the fact that they'll constantly present each other with the kind of challenge that just keeps them going on and on together. They'll always have something to say to and learn from one another, and that will keep this fire alive.

In bed: Imagine the scene. The lusty Sagittarius woman meets the insatiable Scorpio man; Fire meets Water. Things get seriously hot and steamy until the sexual passions are boiling over! This is not for the fainthearted and neither is likely to feel the slightest hint of indifference. The Scorpio man's preference is to drag the Sagittarius woman back to his dark and dangerous den for some deeply erotic experiences, while she'll be dreaming about taking him by the hand to a mountaintop to make love under the stars until dawn. If he had his way, she'd probably end up handcuffed to the bedpost and if she had her way, they'd be swinging from the treetops. They both really want each other like mad, but they also both want the other to do it their way like mad. There are many features of their sex life that will make this affair an exotic, erotic heaven, but there's one issue that will be more difficult to deal with, and that is that the Sagittarius woman will find it near-impossible to accept Scorpio's jealousy. For the Sagittarius lady needs freedom and just can't give the Scorpio man the security and total commitment he requires. In the long term, Scorpio's demands could make it difficult to sustain great sex while the Sagittarius lady's absence will make sex nonexistent. Mutual trust, however, could help to keep the thrust of this relationship going.

SAGITTARIUS WOMAN WITH **SAGITTARIUS MAN**

In love: How could these two not find each other fascinating, exciting, and lovable? They've both found their perfect traveling companion and that equates to life partner, for whether they travel to far-off lands or to wondrous places inside their heads, both are on a constant journey of discovery. They're on the same wavelength, and even if they're not physically in each other's presence, there will always be an intimate connection between them. When they're in the same city, they'll often be spotted jogging side by side through the park or on adjacent running machines at the gym, and they'll be smiling at each other as they listen to music through their twin headphones attached to one MP3 player. They inspire and urge one another on to reach new heights and to go beyond everyone else's expectations. It's true that they may get caught up in a world that's somewhat unreal and exaggerated, but it'll feel good and neither will ever choose the mundane again once they've seen the potential they show one another. Nor will one mind if the other needs to fly solo for a while because they know that the return will be fabulous and that it will be accompanied by exciting, encouraging, and delightful tales of adventure. Two Sagittarians together will certainly share many late-night philosophical discussions or moments when they roll about laughing trying to see who can tell the best joke or come up with the ultimate funny anecdote. Neither is the type that needs to have the last word so, win or lose, they'll both come first with each other.

In bed: This is a pair of red-hot daredevils! They're both hot to trot, so there's never a dull moment when two Archers get together. Both express their sexual desire with a lusty, unself-conscious enthusiasm, but there's always the fun of the chase to be enjoyed before they lock their legs around each other. Two Sagittarians together are like a pair of randy horses frolicking in a field. First the mare will sidle up to the stallion, swishing her tail in his direction then, just as he's about to grab her, she'll gallop away so that he follows. After this happens a few times, he gets wise and may even ignore her, so the next time she'll have to hang about a bit longer to really grab his attention. That's when he gets tensed and ready, and she'll enjoy the moment of erotic delight that she's been waiting for. That's what it's sometimes like for these two Sagittarians. One night, they'll play about like the horses in the field, but the next, their lovemaking will be intense and passionate. These two lovers will never get bored with the fun they share in the bedroom; they could go on and on for they both have an insatiable appetite for every experience. They have the kind of libido that can be sparked off with the slightest encouragement, so these spontaneous, sexually charged creatures are likely to get the urge anywhere, anytime. But they'll have to be careful not to get caught in a compromising situation when they're out and about—unless, of course, they're into that kind of thing!

SAGITTARIUS WOMAN WITH **CAPRICORN MAN**

In love: A very deep bond can develop between the Sagittarius woman and the Capricorn man. He's very attracted to her warmth, optimism, and willingness to live life to the full and she has an interesting way of looking at the world, which he finds to be both inspiring and enlightening. She, for her part, will be extremely susceptible to his ironic sense of humor, his intense physical energy, and his natural wisdom concerning both the world as a whole and his personal life. These two can do amazing things together because they both aspire to something higher— a spiritual and creative life. She'll feed him the ideas and wild dreams and show him their potential, and he'll make them reality. When they are together, their lives can be very productive, creative, and fulfilling, with the love between them arising from their respect for and admiration of one another. The relationship might not live up to Lady Sagittarius's ideal of romance and may not offer her the freedom to roam about as she pleases, but it is certainly the next best thing. The Capricorn man will have to devote a certain amount of his energy toward taming her, but that will help to keep the energy flowing between them. If she needs an occasional night out or a weekend away with the girls, then he's pragmatic enough not to stop her, but as soon as she's home, she'd better be prepared to be wooed by a moody man because the lack of physical contact will have left him feeling a bit depressed.

In bed: The horny Goat really wants to get down and get sexy— and all the time. He's not fussy about where or when they do it, and neither is she, so long as they get on with it! The Capricorn man has a tendency to behave a bit as though he were a teacher, so he can't help but want to teach his Sagittarius lady his new dimension to lovemaking, and she makes a very attentive student. But things aren't all one-sided; she'll show him a thing or two about red-hot passion. She'll be so mad with anticipation that the Capricorn man will simply have to follow her lead. That's just what she wants but will he mind that she's managed to gain control? Can he stop her? Maybe not, but he'll do his best to get into the driving seat. Sometimes their erotic adventures will give them a long leisurely ride at a comfortable pace, allowing them to take in all the subtleties as they go. Other times it will be a hilariously bumpy, boisterous, fun-filled jaunt, over rough-and-tumble territory. But mostly it will seem like a thrillingly paced grand prix; there'll be very few pit stops, and they'll be sweating from exertion and completely exhausted as they race across the finish line. And then they'll have the popping corks and spurting champagne to enjoy as well. This is a winning combination in the bedroom at least, if nowhere else.

SAGITTARIUS WOMAN WITH **AQUARIUS MAN**

In love: There's a natural affinity between the Sagittarius woman and the Aquarius man. She'll give him all the freedom and independence that he wants and will support his solo endeavors.

For his part, he won't restrict her desire to explore and experience life to her heart's content. Each has a deep respect for the other's need for fulfillment as an individual, so a loving bond will grow between them as they realize what a rare and special person they have found and how much rarer and more special they have become as a result of their alliance. This is a relationship where they can be fully themselves. There's no need to put on airs and graces to impress each other; he loves her just the way she is and vice versa. He won't buy her flowers or whisper sweet nothings in her ear, but neither will he be insincere or untruthful about what she means to him. The Aquarius man's love is honest and friendly. They can't fail to inspire wondrous new thoughts and ideas in each other and will really connect and grow into one another, so much so that, on evenings when they were just going to sit and have a little chat, by the time they think about going to bed, the sun will be high in the sky. Their excitement at indulging so wholeheartedly in fascinating, mind-expanding conversations is such that the air will crackle around them. They'll never get bored with each other unless she's the type of Sagittarius who's addicted to the gym or he's the type of Aquarius man who's married to his computer.

In bed: The cool Aquarius man doesn't take long to warm up when a hot Sagittarius lady is giving him the eye, but he may be a bit taken aback by her open, unself-conscious way of expressing her sexual desire. He can't quite believe that his fantasy woman is actually there next to him, in the flesh! But will he be able to tame this wild, wanton creature? Does he really want to? She certainly gets his eroticism going and she'll find that he makes love as much with his mind as with his body. Her fiery, adventurous nature inspires him to try ever more different ways of bringing her pleasure. She'll test his inventiveness to the limit, which is exactly what he needs to stay interested, so together they'll discover some truly unusual ways to make love. He can be a touch selfish but the idea is that if she watches him, she'll be encouraged to do the same—a mutual turn-on! When he puts in a particularly good performance, the type that has her screaming "encore," he might get a little cocky, but she'll take control of the situation and they'll soon be rocking the night away, then singing like canaries once again with the rising sun.

SAGITTARIUS WOMAN WITH **PISCES MAN**

 In love: There's an unreal quality to the attraction between the Pisces man and the Sagittarius woman. They both have their own individual way of looking at life as if through a magnifying glass. One of them will be examining what they say, the other what they do, but whichever area of their life is under the microscope, it will have an alluring and hypnotic appeal. It can also be completely infuriating! One thing is sure, though; they won't fail to fascinate and flow around one another. When they actually connect and enter the physical realm, however, it might feel as though something doesn't quite live up to its promise. Then they'll try again, and again, dancing a strange dance that never ends or, in some cases, never truly satisfies. This could spiral upward into a heavenly waltz that inspires them and gives them something to aspire to, or it may go in the opposite direction and feel like a hellish jive on broken glass. They both encourage the other's pursuits, but because they jump to their own conclusions as to what's really going on, they may simply encourage each other in completely the wrong direction. That's when they could start blaming each other for their own mistakes; she'll ride roughshod over his sensitivity and he'll refuse to be hooked by responsibility. When this relationship is good, it feels as if there's not only a heart, mind, and body connection, but an irresistible spiritual bond as well. But when it's not so good, it might be better if the romantic Mr. Fish swam away and the Lady Archer aimed her arrows of love at another target.

In bed: There's no doubt about it, this is a sexy, steamy, saucy, sweet, and extremely sensual entanglement. It will be whatever they both dream it to be. Both have vast imaginations that are capable of making even the most ordinary situation into a real-life fairytale. They'll immerse themselves in the moment and get fired up and carried away on a fantastical journey, only to return to reality with nothing to show for their journey and not at all sure where they've been. The Pisces man is after an emotional link when he indulges in the pleasures of the flesh, and he'll strive to find and maintain one, but Lady Sagittarius simply doesn't have the emotional staying power he needs. She may not be able to provide the soft, lovey-dovey doe-eyed looks that really limber up his libido and satisfy his longing. Instead, she'll offer him a well of ecstasy to dive into and lose himself in, but while he's in there swimming around and looking to bring back that loving feeling, she'll be off on a wild sexual tangent, leaving him a little at a loss as to how to catch her. That's when it wouldn't be a good idea for him to flop about like a fish out of water just because things aren't perfect. A Sagittarius lady needs a firm sense of direction and won't be happy if she's left to travel the path to erotic bliss all on her own.

THE **SAGITTARIUS MAN** IN LOVE

The Sagittarius man won't easily be pinned down by love. Lust, on the other hand, will drive him to forge relationships here, there, and everywhere. When he meets a woman whom he genuinely enjoys spending time with, exploring philosophical ideas with, or talking with about the oddities of culture in some off-the-beaten-track foreign land that he's just visited, then he can't get her to bed fast enough. He's an opportunist in the nicest sense of the word because opportunities always afford him fresh knowledge, new understanding, and rich experiences. But he's a man who likes to keep his options open. Every time he chooses to commit himself to one person, he's painfully aware that he's cutting himself off from the chance to be openly involved sexually, mentally, or spiritually with all the other interesting and attractive women he meets. This is the fact that any woman who gets involved with a Sagittarius man must face. He's an inclusive person by nature so, while she can be happy in the knowledge that if he's sleeping with her, he genuinely likes her and finds her beautiful, intelligent, and interesting, she might not be quite so sure that he doesn't also include a bunch of other beautiful, intelligent, and interesting women in his life. If, however, he makes the ultimate commitment of sharing his personal space with her or marrying her, then there should be no doubt in her mind that he truly loves her and that there's no other woman for him. By agreeing so publicly to an exclusive relationship with her, he's proved that she's worth more to him than all the other relationships he's ever had or that might be available to him in the future.

Despite this and regardless of the commitment he's made, the Sagittarius man will continue to express his desire for freedom. He won't always consult his partner or think of asking her permission when he wants to head off on one of his voyages of discovery to a distant land, or even when he simply goes off to the local library, café, or gym. He'll probably invite her along, but if she has other plans he won't mind; he'll simply kiss her, tell her to enjoy herself, and wave goodbye. And just as he expects her to allow him his freedom, so he's equally encouraging of her need to express herself freely. He won't try to restrict or sabotage her choices and he doesn't want to control her; instead he embraces her desire to reach her own potential without his interference or assistance. To some women that might seem as though he doesn't care enough to help, but to others it's all the help they could possibly want for it shows his confidence in her ability to achieve things on her own.

This man dislikes romance in the conventional sense. There won't be many cozy candlelit dinners or heart-shaped cards on Valentine's Day. Instead he'll offer trips into the wilderness on the back of a fast motorbike so that the two of them can be inspired by the mating rituals of wild horses, or long walks on a sandy beach to discuss the merits of, well, anything under the sun. This is the Sagittarius man's own special brand of romance. It can lead to an embracing, playful, and warm expression of love that's as spontaneous as it is passionate.

SAGITTARIUS MAN WITH **ARIES WOMAN**

In love: These two could fall in love at first sight. It's as though they both immediately recognize the fact that they share an adventurous, questing spirit—one that puts a fire in their hearts that makes them live, love, and lust with sweet abandon. However, the Sagittarius man is known for his wandering. She will adore being his intrepid traveling companion as he wanders over her body, but if he wanders in the direction of someone else's, it's unlikely to amuse the usually game Aries woman. She demands to be his one and only! And the truth is, she has all that this man could or would ever want from a life partner. He's amazed at her willingness to face obstacles head on and at her display of resilience as she picks herself up with a smile and a wave when life has momentarily got her down. She is intrigued by the way he embraces the philosophical and the spiritual: he has the capacity to broaden her mind, feed her hungry soul, and enhance her spiritual awareness at a physical and emotional level. However, while they both enjoy a good laugh, they should tone down the energy levels and be sensitive to other people's need for peace if they want to keep their friends. Once these two make a commitment to one another, life will never be the same again, but who wants a past when there's such a bright future?

In bed: The twinkle in his eye tells her that she's in for the ride of her life! The fire in hers lets him know that he'd better do something about it now or he'll lose her forever. They know they want one another as soon as they set eyes on each other, but this burning passion will need to be tamed or else it could rage out of all control in a very short period of time. She'll inspire him to be fast on his feet, and he'll keep her on her toes while they're both head over heels. They both laugh a lot and know how to have a good time. Everyone knows that laughter is the best medicine, but they need to be careful that they don't overdose! This is a pairing with lifelong potential but to make it last, they should pace themselves. Time is not important for either of these signs, and anything is possible when the Aries woman and Sagittarius man get passionate. Fire and fire together make an inferno of unadulterated excitement. Imagine the scene...they're at her best friend's wedding and the bride lends the Aries girl the key to her honeymoon suite so she can pop up and freshen up her makeup. The Sagittarius man, ever the opportunist, follows. Spontaneity is the name of his game.

SAGITTARIUS MAN WITH **TAURUS WOMAN**

In love: The Taurus woman will find the Sagittarius man intriguing and esthetically pleasing, but this relationship will take some serious work. If she looks upon him as a project, she'll find her work cut out, and if she expects to slot into his life just like that, she'll be surprised to discover that it's not that easy. He will find her soothing manner comforting to come home to, but she will have to tolerate his need to be a free spirit. In other words, he won't come home very often! She'll find it almost impossible to rely on his time-keeping. He may say that he'll be home at five, but that could mean five in the morning, or even in five days' time! Since Taurus is a Fixed sign, she prefers to make plans, but they all go out the window when she tries to make them with a Sagittarius man. One of their basic differences is that he finds it hard to relax and stay in one place, while she might find it hard to be spontaneous. These two are fundamentally different, but if they can get past the first hurdle and if the Taurus woman can learn not to be too offended by the wild Sagittarius man's wayward adventuring, lack of tact, and outspokenness, then love can develop between them. This is a union that will take time and effort to settle but if they both give a little and are prepared to meet halfway, it could be an enlightening experience for both of them.

In bed: In a nutshell, the luxurious Taurus woman is expensive, while the adventurous Sagittarius man is expansive—which is not such a bad thing! For the Taurus woman, being in bed with a Sagittarius man is like being with someone from a completely different background and culture—he's like a foreigner in her land. It takes a bit of getting used to, but it can be very exotic. Once she sees how he glows when she parades around the bedroom in her brand new upmarket lingerie, it will be obvious that this holiday romance has serious potential. He's a lusty traveler who enjoys being on the move all over her body. He's also into learning, and if he has to spend all night studying every little bit of her, he'll happily do it—and he won't mind revising at regular intervals. She is as unembarrassed as he is when it comes to displays of physical desire, all of which he finds very sexy and appealing—shrinking violets are not his thing. However, should she ever try to tie him down for too long—even if it's with a pair of silk stockings to the bedstead—then his mind will start wandering, and with it his libido!

SAGITTARIUS MAN WITH **GEMINI WOMAN**

 In love: This pairing is a case of "opposites attract." She's all about finding diversity and he's searching for a unifying theme. Together they'll be deep into endless debate, lively conversation, challenging mental gymnastics, and practical jokes. The Gemini woman can't help but love the Sagittarius guy. She finds the intellectual expansion that comes from spending time with him a powerful incitement to love. She can't possibly fall for anyone who doesn't turn her on mentally, and since this guy doesn't just turn her on, but also turns her inside out and upside down as well, she'll tumble straight into his arms. He watches her with an Archer's eye, delighting in the challenge she presents. She never reveals a target he can pin her down to for very long, but if anyone can nail her, he will. They're a match, that's for sure, fitting together like a hand in a glove. Even when one gets irritable and wants some space, the other won't hesitate to allow it and will back off graciously. Neither is clingy or possessive, and they both need their space so they will respect the other's need; they'll each just go and explore another landscape but wouldn't dream of questioning the other's loyalty—well, at least not beyond normal expectations. They have different motivations, but similar intentions. He'll make her laugh until she cries, but that just fuels her exhilaration. As they dance around each other, their feelings will be woven into a pattern of love that touches the very fabric of their souls.

 In bed: Whooaaa! Bring along the riding crop and giddy-up! Need we say more? Talk about insatiable appetites! No one would believe what goes on behind this couple's closed doors. Their antics would leave anyone watching either in a state of shocked disbelief or feeling inspired to spice up their own love life. What they'd see wouldn't really be any more lewd than average, it's just that the raucous, sometimes acrobatic, burlesque revelry that goes on while these two are making love is truly amazing! The Sagittarius man, for all his high-minded ideals, still has enough of the wild animal about him to teach his Gemini lover to unleash the fantasies that she never knew she had. Her planetary ruler, Mercury, has wings on his feet, but nothing could prepare her for the sexual terrain she can cover riding on a Centaur. He'll take her to heaven and back again. She's a nimble little minx, though, and can stay with him through all their athletic exertions for as long as he can keep it up. He'll love her thighs so stockings are a prerequisite, and if she squeezes his flanks between them, he'll happily submit to her directions. These two not only adore one another in a romantic sense, they also have amazing fun.

SAGiTTARiUS MAN WiTH **CANCER WOMAN**

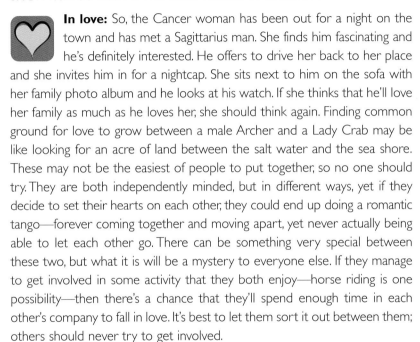

In love: So, the Cancer woman has been out for a night on the town and has met a Sagittarius man. She finds him fascinating and he's definitely interested. He offers to drive her back to her place and she invites him in for a nightcap. She sits next to him on the sofa with her family photo album and he looks at his watch. If she thinks that he'll love her family as much as he loves her, she should think again. Finding common ground for love to grow between a male Archer and a Lady Crab may be like looking for an acre of land between the salt water and the sea shore. These may not be the easiest of people to put together, so no one should try. They are both independently minded, but in different ways, yet if they decide to set their hearts on each other, they could end up doing a romantic tango—forever coming together and moving apart, yet never actually being able to let each other go. There can be something very special between these two, but what it is will be a mystery to everyone else. If they manage to get involved in some activity that they both enjoy—horse riding is one possibility—then there's a chance that they'll spend enough time in each other's company to fall in love. It's best to let them sort it out between them; others should never try to get involved.

In bed: This is another relationship that combines the elements of Fire and Water. Sometimes the result is a huge explosion of sexual chemistry but at other times it's just a pile of wet soot! If they don't annoy each other they'll have a ton of boiling hot steam between them. Theirs will be an unforgettable experience even if they'd both prefer to put it out of their minds. It's also unrepeatable, which could be good or bad, depending on the peculiarities of the particular Sagittarius man and Cancer woman. Many couples born under these signs—those with a seriously good sense of humor—will have a healthy, happy, and fulfilling sex life together. They'll have a rip-roaring time with plenty of romping and stomping. In fact, this liaison can be downright tempestuous, as they burn up many calories in pursuit of each other. But it will also have an element of danger, which they'll either love or hate. Most Cancer women are too sensitive and clingy for the free-spirited and often tactless Sagittarius man, but if she withdraws into her shell, he'll think that's the signal for him to go off adventuring in new territory.

SAGiTTARiUS MAN WiTH **LEO WOMAN**

 In love: Since both these two were born under Fire signs, theirs is an uplifting, spirited partnership. The Sagittarius man has lots to offer in terms of glamour and travel and, depending on his mood, he can come up with deep, meaningful conversation or flippant, meaningless chitchat. The Leo woman will easily catch his drift. They're always on the same wavelength and always game for a laugh together. The Sagittarius man easily falls for the Leo woman's warmth, self-assuredness, and generous nature. Her *joie de vivre* is infectious and he sees her as a glittering prize to be won at all costs. He'll focus all his attention and exercise all his skill on sending an arrow of love straight into her heart and will entertain her, wine and dine her, and love her dearly, almost desperately. But as he's an Archer he hunts from a distance, so he won't always reveal his motives in an obvious fashion. He wouldn't want to expose himself or let her think that winning him is easy. He spends a good portion of his time away, either traveling with friends or on business, or simply in the rec room. He's the kind of man who needs his space, and that excites the Leo woman because she loves a man with an independent streak. One thing that will soon become clear is that once these two make a commitment, all his searching, questing, and adventuring will be focused on bringing back treasures to lay at the feet of his lady love. Her heart will soar sky-high with the joy of it all.

In bed: They begin on the same note and follow the same beat, so these two lovers will always have the same rhythm. At the start, there's lots of bass and the vibrations are felt from deep within. Next comes the middle—a perfect harmonic connection followed by top notes sustained until they can't stand it any more! Come the end, they both fall about laughing…then they do it all over again. Neither can get enough; she will love, cherish, and honor every bit of this man, and he loves to see her lose control. He wants to take the reins and be the tour guide on their journey to sexual bliss. Only with this woman to boost the temperature can he blast off into the stratospheric realms he's always dreamed of. When they come down to earth, they'll have such memories that every time they look at each other they'll be planning their next erotic adventure together.

SAGITTARIUS MAN WITH VIRGO WOMAN

In love: The love between a Virgo woman and a Sagittarius man is a strange one. In some ways they're totally compatible and get on really well together. He doesn't want an overly romantic partner, and is impressed by her capability, intelligence, and willingness to lend a hand. She, meanwhile, is stimulated by his philosophical turn of mind and enjoys hearing all about his busy life without becoming jealous. She's a neatness freak, while he doesn't notice when things are messy or out of place, and although she likes things clean and tidy, she doesn't appreciate having to pick up after him. She'll do it because it will drive her crazy to live in his mess, but she could end up resenting him for turning her into a criticizing nag. And if that's the way she behaves over half a dozen dirty coffee cups, then he'll soon fall out of love with her. She'll let him know what she expects but if she goes quiet on him, he could assume that her interest has turned elsewhere —though it might take him a while to notice! This partnership may never really get off the ground and live up to its potential, but there is such a thing as a Sagittarius man who will love and cherish his adorable Virgo lady enough to keep her happy. And she'll certainly be able to keep him happy!

In bed: The playful, adventurous Sagittarius man can be quite a turn-on for the demure, self-contained Lady Virgo. He's a bit of an Indiana Jones-type—a ruggedly masculine, philosophical adventurer, who appeals both to her mind and her libidinous desires. But he's not in the habit of putting a lot of time into building up her passion. One or other of them will have to modify their expectations. If the Virgo lady can learn to initiate more than she normally would, then he'll rise to the occasion faster than a rocket. He's so naturally lusty and spontaneous that he would love her to be ready at a moment's notice for a rumble in the jungle! When she is, it's great between them, but to really have her swinging like a primate, he needs to expend some energy on grooming her. He'll be happy to learn how, just for her benefit, but on those occasions when they just can't get their timing right, she'll be left standing on a precipice with only her own ingenuity to get herself off.

SAGITTARIUS MAN WITH **LIBRA WOMAN**

In love: The Sagittarius man will sweep the Libra woman off her feet, take her on a whirlwind ride and then, hey! Where did he go? But he'll be back, for he sees all that's lovely in her. The problem is that he sees loveliness everywhere and can't help but go and take a closer look! However, when this man commits, he does so wholeheartedly, unlike the Lady Libra, who'll still be weighing up the pros and cons in the relationship until well after the marriage. But she loves him; he has a refined soul and a touch of wildness that thrills and excites her, and he also makes her laugh and feel free to express her true self. He might not always take her views into consideration when he's making a decision and although she'd like him to, he certainly doesn't tell her that he loves her every five minutes. But she knows he does without him telling her, so, to keep the peace that she wants and needs, it's better for her to let him think he has all the freedom in the world. And if he thinks he has, then he'll show her that what he really wants is her! It's true that he suffers from wanderlust and always will, but when he's around, he's so appreciative of all her good qualities that she doesn't mind. And after all, when she stops to think about it, his wanderlust suits the sociable Libra lady perfectly because that leaves her free to spend time with friends, and do a little flirting—which only serves to keep her keen on her Sagittarius man since she'll find that he really is one in a million.

 In bed: This is an energetic relationship—in the bedroom, in the bathroom, in the kitchen, on the stairs, in the garden, on the way home….Things can get hot and heavy between the Libra lady and Sagittarius man just about anytime and anywhere, though "hot and happy" might be a better description, for they have so much fun frolicking about in the bedroom. When she shows him her bright, bubbly side, he can't help but get excited and then there's no stopping him. He won't hold back for nicety's sake and he may not have all the refined, romantic qualities that she desires in a lover, but he's adventurous and so fantastically frisky that his spontaneous streak could catch her unawares at the most awkward moments. But the rough-and-ready Sagittarius man won't mind; he finds her unpreparedness a real turn-on. It brings out the beast in him and makes him wild with passion. Of course, she'll try to tame him, but she's no match for his passion—he'll hunt her down and turn her on beyond the point of no return.

SAGITTARIUS MAN WITH **SCORPIO WOMAN**

In love: The Scorpio woman will be charmed and inspired by the adventurous soul of the Sagittarius man, just as he'll be intrigued and seduced by her controlled intensity. He'll make her laugh at the absurdity of life and will open her mind to new experiences and ideas that will provide her with plenty of mysteries—then he'll beg her to solve them. She'll fascinate him with the depth of her understanding, her way of exploring philosophical ideas from a psychological perspective, and her veiled feminine eroticism that will excite his own sense of masculinity. The attraction between these two is strong and promises not only to be interesting and entertaining, but mind-expanding as well. However, it's a promise that's hard to keep because he can be elusive and she can be possessive, and somehow the two just can't be in a relationship together without him agreeing to have his freedom curtailed or her exercising tighter control on her jealousy. They have such an ardent two-way fascination with each other, however, that it would be difficult for them not to fall in love. They'll explore the deep, dark recesses of each other's fathomless souls and will gradually learn to trust one another, but it may take time, and perhaps more time than either might be willing to give. In the end, the relationship will be worth it if they both recognize the way that their egos keep them apart, and that it's their hearts that matter most. If they follow their hearts, then they'll go all the way.

In bed: The sex life of a Scorpio woman and a Sagittarius man is bound to be steamy! There's such a sexual pressure that builds up when they're together and things can get so intense between them that afterward they'll be picking pieces of each other off the walls, ceiling, and floor. This lusty man enjoys romping with her in bed or in any other place where they happen to be when he's aroused—and she will arouse him! He finds her very sexy indeed; it's almost as if she were weaving a kind of magic spell over him. She has a way of taking him deep inside his wild, animalistic nature; he gets so intoxicated with sensual delight that he behaves like a savage on the rampage—exactly what the Scorpio woman desires. He's adventurous and she's amazingly sensual, so together they'll go along dark alleys, through deep tunnels, then rocket up to the stratosphere. Things might get a little uncomfortable at times, but any place is worth a try! The possibilities are endless so they'll never get bored, even after years of being together. But there's one habit that the Sagittarius man has that the Scorpio lady will have to get used to if she wants to keep the peace: she shouldn't expect him to be there in the morning when she wakes up. He has places to go and people to see.

SAGITTARIUS MAN WITH **SAGITTARIUS WOMAN**

See pages 68–69.

SAGITTARIUS MAN WITH **CAPRICORN WOMAN**

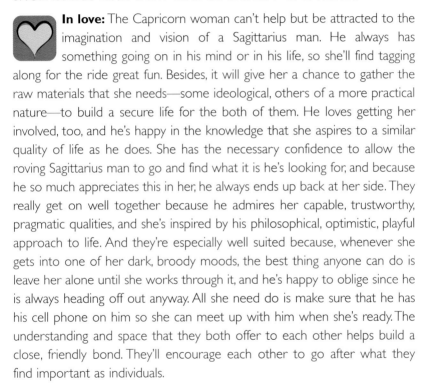

In love: The Capricorn woman can't help but be attracted to the imagination and vision of a Sagittarius man. He always has something going on in his mind or in his life, so she'll find tagging along for the ride great fun. Besides, it will give her a chance to gather the raw materials that she needs—some ideological, others of a more practical nature—to build a secure life for the both of them. He loves getting her involved, too, and he's happy in the knowledge that she aspires to a similar quality of life as he does. She has the necessary confidence to allow the roving Sagittarius man to go and find what it is he's looking for, and because he so much appreciates this in her, he always ends up back at her side. They really get on well together because he admires her capable, trustworthy, pragmatic qualities, and she's inspired by his philosophical, optimistic, playful approach to life. And they're especially well suited because, whenever she gets into one of her dark, broody moods, the best thing anyone can do is leave her alone until she works through it, and he's happy to oblige since he is always heading off out anyway. All she need do is make sure that he has his cell phone on him so she can meet up with him when she's ready. The understanding and space that they both offer to each other helps build a close, friendly bond. They'll encourage each other to go after what they find important as individuals.

In bed: When the Capricorn woman can actually get hold of her Sagittarius guy and get him to make some time for lovemaking, then she'll discover that this is a very lusty man indeed! She responds well to his touch, since physical contact is the foundation that underpins her sexual awakening, while her intense desire communicates itself to him on a primal, instinctive level and fires him up so much that he just loves romping around the bedroom with her. There's something extremely animalistic about this erotic pairing; he'll track down her sexy scent until his nostrils flare and the wild, untamed aspects of his nature take control of him. The Sagittarius man will be something of a bucking bronco so the Capricorn woman may need all the self-control she can muster, but if anyone can get him to jump over hurdles and set the pace for passionate pleasure, then she can. He may, however, have galloped away before she wakes up in the morning, but hopefully it will just be to fetch the coffee, croissants, and Sunday newspapers. And as she is such a sensually charged lady, she'll always be randy and ready for his return. This sexual duo has a lot to recommend it, but the Capricorn lady could get tired of putting her life on hold while waiting for her Sagittarius man to return. He'll need a very long rein but it could serve more than one purpose; she could use it to whip him into shape once she's pulled him in, but she should never try to tie him down!

SAGITTARIUS MAN WITH **AQUARIUS WOMAN**

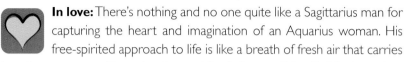

In love: There's nothing and no one quite like a Sagittarius man for capturing the heart and imagination of an Aquarius woman. His free-spirited approach to life is like a breath of fresh air that carries her along on an exciting adventure, while she's everything that he loves in a woman—independent, intelligent, gregarious, and with a unique, nonchalant sex appeal that arouses his longing to know more about her. It just feels so right and easy between them and they bring out the best in each other. They automatically allow each other the space they need to reach their full potential, leaving plenty of room for an honest love to blossom between them. What could possibly go wrong? Well, there's a slight chance that, because they're both out discovering things or saving the world, finding time to be together might prove difficult. The good thing is that the Aquarius woman is about as reasonable as they come and the Sagittarius man will forever fascinate and stimulate her inquiring mind. So long as they keep the channels of communication open and intimacy high on their list of priorities, there'll be no end to their delight in one another. Neither will try to hold the other back; instead they'll nurture each other's aims and ideals. They value the mutual attraction, friendship, and honesty that they share, as well as those frequent occasions when their laughter at the absurdities of life and at each other brings them close. This one is for keeps. This couple born of Fire and Air get on like a house on fire.

In bed: This is one hot-to-trot relationship! She's as innovative and inventive as he's lusty and adventurous, so when they're together, things can get pretty wild. Spontaneity is the name of the game and it's a game that they both want to play. The Sagittarius man and the Aquarius woman could find themselves swinging from the chandelier one minute and sweating over the stove the next. This couple is really cooking and they serve up something very tasty indeed! Any place, any time—morning, noon, or night—and anything and everything goes. The Sagittarius/Aquarius sex life is pure passion. There may be the odd occasion when she needs more foreplay, both verbal and physical, for he has a tendency to silently and stealthily get her in his sights then unexpectedly pierce her with his Archer's arrow, but since there'll be many erotic replays, she'll soon learn to read the signs and be alert to his huntsman's tactics. And she may well use her imagination to reverse the predator–prey roles and lead him on a merry chase around the bedroom.

SAGiTTARiUS mAn WiTH **PiSCES WOmAn**

 In love: The Sagittarius man and Pisces woman will be drawn together by a feeling for the possibility of endless love. "Ordinary" isn't a word that describes either of them, so theirs could be an extraordinary love affair. They'll both enjoy long, fascinating conversations about the meaning of life and about what we're all doing here, but no matter what conclusions they come to, they may not be able to answer the question of why they're together. He doesn't like her getting under his skin, which she'll do in spite of him because he finds her so enticing and intriguing, and although she's hopelessly attracted to his fun-loving, adventurous soul, he's always taking himself off and simply isn't there enough for her. Every time he leaves she feels she has to extricate her heart; he's completely cavalier about her emotions. At first, they'll drive each other crazy with desire but eventually they'll just drive each other crazy. At this point, they'd be wise to stand back and take stock of what there is between them. It's hard to deny that they feel strong passions for each other and that both of them have a leaning toward the spiritual and philosophical. If they can take a few small leaps of faith, then this is a partnership that could have a firm foundation of love, hope, mind, and body, but without some spirit it will be hard to maintain.

In bed: He's a fun guy for a romp in the hay, a tumble in the grass, or a roll in the sack, so she'll never get bored with the scenery when she's frolicking around with a Sagittarius man. But sex for the Pisces woman isn't always a picnic. She's the romantic type who needs all the pretty trimmings to achieve true satisfaction. When they get together between the sheets, she'd like a little more emotional connection. He'll give her something of what she needs but the experience may be shorter lived than she expects! He's not really the luxuriating type; although he'll be seduced by her soft, languorous sensuality, he isn't very subtle in expressing his arousal. She wants to feel his passion, deeply, and is excited by his obvious desire for her, but while she's happy to give herself up to him, she won't like having her feelings trampled on. These two can enjoy their sexy fun and games as long as the sun shines, but should be ready to pack up when they see the dark clouds approaching. But this on–off thing doesn't have to end there if they can accept the dynamic of their immense sexual desire and capacity for one another, and treat it like an ever-changing, developing part of their relationship. In fact, neither of them would ever get bored and things would simply get better.